A Guide for Using

Anne Frank

The Diary of a Young Girl

in the Classroom

Based on the book written by Anne Frank

*This guide written by **Mari Lu Robbins**
and illustrated by **Agi Palinay***

Teacher Created Materials, Inc.
6421 Industry Way
Westminster, CA 92683
www.teachercreated.com
©*1996 Teacher Created Materials*
Reprinted, 2001, a
Made in U.S.A.
ISBN 1-55734-559-7

Edited by
Cathy Gilbert

Cover Art by
Wendy Chang

The classroom teacher may reproduce copies of materials in this book for classroom use only. The reproduction of any part for an entire school or school system is strictly prohibited. No part of this publication may be transmitted, stored, or recorded in any form without written permission from the publisher.

Table of Contents

Introduction 3

Sample Lesson Plans 4

Before the Book (*Pre-reading Activities*) 5

About the Author 6

Book Summary 7

Vocabulary Lists 8

Vocabulary Activity Ideas 9

Section 1 (*Introduction through Friday, 21 August, 1942*) 10
- ❖ Quiz Section 1
- ❖ Hands-on Project—*Make a Time Line of the World's Major Religions*
- ❖ Cooperative Learning Activity—*Anticipation Guide*
- ❖ Curriculum Connection—*Judaism: Anne Frank's Religion A Short Story of Nazi Germany;*
- ❖ Into Your Life—*Reading Response Journals*

Section 2 (*Wednesday, 2 September, 1942, through Thursday, 25 March, 1943*) 17
- ❖ Quiz Section 2
- ❖ Hands-on Project—*Draw Anne's Room*
- ❖ Cooperative Learning Activity—*Being in Hiding*
- ❖ Curriculum Connections—*Propaganda and Advertising*
- ❖ Into Your Life—*Write a Letter to Anne*

Section 3 (*Saturday 27, March, 1943, through Saturday, 27 November, 1943*) 23
- ❖ Quiz Section 3
- ❖ Hands-on Project—*Greek and Roman Mythology*
- ❖ Cooperative Learning Activity—*Radio Journalism*
- ❖ Curriculum Connection—*The Holocaust*
- ❖ Into Your Life—*Prepare an Escape Bag*

Section 4 (*Monday, 6 December, 1943, through Friday, 31 March, 1944*) 29
- ❖ Quiz Section 4
- ❖ Hands-on Project—*Start a Photo Collection*
- ❖ Cooperative Learning Activity—*Writing Proverbs*
- ❖ Curriculum Connection—*Write a News Story*
- ❖ Into Your Life—*Heroes and Teachers*

Section 5 (*Monday 3 April, 1944 through Tuesday, 1 August, 1944*) 34
- ❖ Quiz Section 5
- ❖ Hands-on Project—*Coping with Food Cycles*
- ❖ Cooperative Learning Activity—*Put Hitler on Trial*
- ❖ Curriculum Connection—*Diphtheria: An Old Scourge; Immunizations*
- ❖ Into Your Life—*The Final Day in the Secret Annexe*

After the Book (*Post-reading Activities*)
- Any Questions? 41
- Research Ideas 42

Culminating Activity 43

Unit Test Options 44

Bibliography of Related Reading 46

Answer Key 47

Introduction

Good books are plentiful, but seldom has a book had the overwhelming effect on the minds of millions of people as this one written as a personal diary by a young girl. The impact of this book and its power to affect the conscience of the world are far beyond the dream of the girl who wrote it so that something of herself would live on.

In *Literature Units,* we take great care to select books that will become treasured friends for life. This is one of those books. Teachers using this unit will find the following features to supplement their own valuable ideas.

- Sample Lesson Plans

- Pre-reading Activities

- A Biographical Sketch of the Author

- A Book Summary

- Vocabulary Lists and Suggested Vocabulary Ideas

- Chapters grouped for study, with each section including a(n):

  —quiz

  —hands-on project

  —cooperative learning activity

  —cross-curricular connection

  —extension into the reader's own life

- Post-reading Activities

- A Culminating Activity

- Two Different Options for Unit Tests

- Bibliography of Related Reading

- Answer Key

We are confident that this unit will be a valuable addition to your literature planning and that as you use our ideas, your students will learn to treasure the life and wisdom of the young girl whose short life and towering dreams fill this book.

Sample Lesson Plans

Each of the lessons suggested below can take from one to several days to complete.

Lesson 1 (Pre-reading)
- Introduce and complete pre-reading activities. (page 5)
- Read "About the Author" with students. (page 6)
- Discuss what it would be like to have to go into hiding with your family if your life is threatened because of your religious beliefs.
- Begin journals and introduce the idea of structured responses to reading.
- Complete the Anticipation Guide. (page 12)
- Introduce vocabulary list for Section 1. (page 8)

Lesson 2 (Introduction through Friday, 21 August, 1942)
- Read Section 1. Place the vocabulary words in context and discuss their meanings.
- Choose a vocabulary activity. (page 9)
- Research the major religions of the world and place their origins on a time line. (page 11)
- Learn about Anne Frank's religion, Judaism. (page 13)
- Administer quiz for Section 1. (page 10)
- Introduce vocabulary list for Section 2. (page 8)

Lesson 3 (Wednesday, 2 September, 1942, through Thursday, 25 March, 1943)
- Read Section 2. Place the vocabulary words in context and discuss their meanings.
- Choose a vocabulary activity. (page 9)
- Draw Anne's room from her description of it. (page 18)
- Complete role play of hiding from the Gestapo. (page 19)
- Learn about the history of Nazi Germany. (pages 20–21)
- Write a letter of advice to Anne. (page 22)
- Administer quiz for Section 2. (page 17)
- Introduce vocabulary for Section 3. (page 8)

Lesson 4 (Saturday, 27 March, 1943, through Saturday, 27 November, 1943)
- Read Section 3. Place the vocabulary words in context and discuss their meanings.
- Choose a vocabulary activity. (page 9)
- Make masks of the Greek gods and goddesses. (page 24)
- Produce a radio show with the occupants of the Secret Annexe sitting around listening to it. (page 25)

- Learn about the Holocaust. (page 26)
- Make an escape bag. (page 28)
- Administer quiz for Section 3. (page 23)
- Introduce vocabulary for Section 4. (page 8)

Lesson 5 (Monday, 6 December, 1943, through Friday, 31 March, 1944)
- Read Section 4. Place the vocabulary words in context and discuss their meanings.
- Choose a vocabulary activity. (page 9)
- Compile a photo collection. (page 30)
- Learn how to write proverbs. (page 31)
- Learn about journalism and writing the news. (page 32)
- Write about heroes and teachers. (page 33)
- Administer quiz for Section 4. (page 29)
- Introduce vocabulary list for Section 5. (page 8)

Lesson 6 (Monday, 3 April, 1944 through Tuesday, 1 August, 1944)
- Read Section 5. Place the vocabulary words in context and discuss their meanings.
- Choose a vocabulary activity. (page 9)
- Learn to cope with food cycles. (page 35)
- Put Hitler on trial. (page 36)
- Learn about immunizations. (page 38)
- Write a diary entry which Anne might have written about her final day in the Secret Annexe. (page 40)
- Administer quiz for Section 5. (page 34)

Lesson 7
- Discuss any questions students may have about the story. (page 41)
- Re-administer anticipation guide.
- Assign book research projects. (page 42)
- Begin work on the culminating activity. (page 44)

Lesson 8
- Administer unit test 1 or 2. (pages 44, 45)
- Discuss test answers and responses.
- Discuss students' enjoyment of the book.
- Provide a list of related readings. (page 46)

Lesson 9
- Complete culminating activity to remember Anne by creating a museum in her honor. (page 43)

4 ©1996 Teacher Created Materials, Inc.

Before the Book

Before you begin reading *Anne Frank: The Diary of A Young Girl,* do some pre-reading activities with your students to stimulate their interest, enhance their comprehension, and help them get an understanding of the time period and cultural framework in which the story is set. Here are some activities that might work well with your class.

1. Predict what the story might be about by hearing the title and looking at the cover illustration.

2. Discuss what the story might be about after reading About the Author (page 6) and Book Summary (page 7).

3. Answer these questions.

   —What do you know about World War II?

   —What do you know about Hitler and Nazi Germany?

   —Are you interested in

      stories about real teenagers?

      stories that reveal cruelty and injustice?

      stories about real-life heroes?

      stories about real people who demonstrate great courage and wisdom?

      stories about real teenagers who must cope with evil?

   —Would you ever

      treat persons badly because of their race or religion?

      be able to spend over two years hiding in an attic?

      allow others to destroy your life because they do not like your religion?

      want to change historical events?

4. Describe a situation in which you or someone you know experienced prejudice.

5. Consider reading the Afterword in the book before beginning the book in order to have a better historical perspective about the time in which Anne Frank lived.

6. Complete the Anticipation Guide (page 12) and discuss the reasons students have the answers they did.

7. Discuss the issues of racial, religious, and ethnic prejudice and discrimination. Why do some people hate others just because they are different? How do some people attempt to force their own beliefs on others? How could a large country relinquish power to a group of cruel and hateful bigots?

About the Author

Anne Frank was born June 12, 1929, in Frankfurt on the Main, Germany, to a prominent family in the city. Her father, Otto Frank, was a highly respected Jewish businessman whose family had lived and worked in Frankfurt for over two hundred years. Anne's early years were spent in relative affluence. Her secure days were filled with loving parents, relatives, and all the benefits of having enough of everything.

In 1933, when Adolf Hitler, with his violent anti-Jewish beliefs, became the dictator of Germany, Otto Frank moved his family to the Netherlands. This tiny country had long been a haven for refugees from other countries, and Mr. Frank hoped that there they would be safe from Hitler's Nazi troops. They were safe for several years, and Anne grew up as a Dutch girl, attending the Montessori School, going to carefree parties, riding her bicycle, laughing and having fun. She had escaped from a country which had as its stated policy a hatred of Jews and a determination to kill all of them.

When Germany invaded Holland in 1940, all of this changed. Jews in Holland were made to wear a yellow Star of David so they would be marked as "different" from non-Jews, were forbidden to go to school with non-Jewish children, and were forbidden to do almost anything while the conquering government set about to arrest all the Jews and ship them off to Germany to be slave laborers and to die. This was when Otto Frank established, with the help of Dutch friends, what they came to call the "Secret Annexe," where the family and four others would spend their last two years of freedom.

The family was betrayed in August, 1944, and all of the people in the Secret Annexe were arrested and shipped off in the last shipment which left from Holland to a concentration camp in Poland. Otto Frank worked as a slave laborer for eight months and survived the war. All of the other inhabitants of the Secret Annexe died in captivity. Anne and her sister, Margot, died of typhus in the Bergen-Belsen concentration camp in late February or early March of 1945, barely two or three months before the end of the war in Europe. It is believed Anne maintained her cheerfulness until the end.

 ©1996 Teacher Created Materials, Inc.

Anne Frank: The Diary of a Young Girl

(Doubleday, 1952)

(Available in Canada, Doubleday Dell Seal; UK, Bantam Doubleday Dell; Australia, Transworld Publishers)

Anne Frank: The Diary of a Young Girl is the real diary of a real girl who lived only fifteen short years during a traumatic period of the world's history. In her small book, she managed to leave her hopes, dreams, fears, and indomitable personality as a never-to-be-forgotten legacy for the world. To anyone who thinks that one person cannot make a difference, this book sends a resounding, "Yes, one can!" Anne Frank lives on in the memory of anyone who once reads what she had to say.

Anne's diary begins on her thirteenth birthday when she is given the journal full of blank pages as a birthday present, and it continues until mere hours before Anne, her family, and the other members of their "Secret Annexe" are arrested by the Gestapo. We have the privilege of seeing inside Anne's mind and soul when we read this book. Through this diary, which she calls Kitty, Anne confides totally in us. She tells us of her dreams and hopes, and she shows us her adolescent petulance and confusions. She tells us her loves and her hates, and she philosophizes about what it is to be human.

We feel Anne's longings to be outside her attic home and her love of nature. We are privy to her first kiss, and we cringe at the thought of eating rotten potatoes or nothing but beans for days. We empathize with her impatience at having to share a tiny bedroom with a middle-aged dentist, and we laugh at her characterizations of the Annexe's other inhabitants, even when they are tinged with the unfairness of adolescence. We say "Of course!" when she confides she wants to be a writer when she grows up, and we grieve that someone so promising should have contributed only one entry into the literature of the world.

Anne wanted to leave something of herself to live on after she was dead, and she left this book. In the four decades since it was first published, Anne's diary has sold many millions of copies and been published in many languages. It has been made into a play and then into a film. She would have liked that, for she collected movie magazines and had a large collection of film star photos on the walls of her room. The building in which the eight inhabitants of the Secret Annexe hid for over two years, stifling their sounds of life and cringing at every unfamiliar noise, is now a museum. Anne got her greatest wish, for as long as there are people to read her diary, she will, indeed, live on.

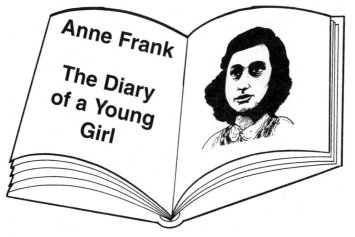

Vocabulary Lists

Section 1 *(Introduction through Friday, 21 August, 1942)*

occupation	melancholy	fanatic	chattel
degradation	capitulation	cum laude	monotonous
poignant	tram	vital	lumbago
appropriate	placard	superfluous	pique
enhance	florin	accord	hypochondria
pogrom	Zionism	concentration	wardrobe

Section 2 *(Wednesday, 2 September, 1942, through Thursday, 25 March, 1943)*

ludicrous	saboteur	pretext	incoherent
surreptitious	vile	ingenuity	rebuke
reprimand	herald	exquisite	dejected
disposition	persevere	penetrate	fatalistic
improvise	congenial	economy	procure
Gestapo	rendezvous	inquisitive	neutrality

Section 3 *(Saturday, 27 March, 1943, through Saturday, 27 November, 1943)*

abdominal	extremity	revocable	Chanuka
incendiary	respective	incessant	palpitation
clandestine	proficient	communal	tranquility
oculist	coquetry	reconciliator	recede
pedantic	figurative	prospectus	diphtheria
smolder	concertina	perturb	condole

Section 4 *(Monday, 6 December, 1943, through Friday, 31 March, 1944)*

brooch	pensive	compensation	adroit
subjective	genealogical	superficial	estrangement
fatuous	furbelow	impertinent	indignation
patronage	plantation	despondent	disparage
brusque	black market	perish	speculate
diligent	solace	nonchalance	sabotage

Section 5 *(Monday, 3 April, 1944, through Tuesday, 1 August, 1944)*

expedient	jocular	epistle	incalculable
scandalous	ardent	boisterous	explicit
liberation	succulent	pedestal	dregs
pseudonym	prefabricated	inflation	devastate
lozenge	capitalist	chaos	
malaria	surpluses	prophecy	
dungarees	persistent	abyss	

8 ©*1996 Teacher Created Materials, Inc.*

Vocabulary Activity Ideas

The vocabulary selected from *Anne Frank: The Diary of a Young Girl* has been divided into five sections. For each section you may wish to have students work together in cooperative learning groups to locate the vocabulary words and define them according to their context in the book.

Providing students with interesting vocabulary activities helps them to understand the meanings of the words. In this way they are more able to integrate the words into their everyday language. Here are some suggestions for activities you might try using with your students. Be sure that students always use the same meaning as are used in the book for these activities.

1. Have students keep a **personal vocabulary diary.** Tell them to record any words which are new to them along with the page number on which the words are found. Have them bring the words to class to review with their classmates within the contexts in which the words are found. Along with the definitions, have the students write a sentence using each word in the diary.

2. Each day have several words as **words of the day.** List the words on the chalkboard or on chart paper at the front of the class and as a warm-up activity, have them use a dictionary to locate the meanings of the words.

3. Have the students play **vocabulary charades** in which they act out the meanings of the words.

4. Have students play **vocabulary categories** in which they create a chart sorting the words into nouns, verbs, adjectives, and adverbs. After the words are listed on the chart, discuss how words often have multiple meanings and how you can tell which meaning a word has by how it is used in a sentence.

5. Write sentences leaving blanks where the vocabulary words belong. Tell students to **use context clues** to complete the sentences.

6. Have students **write a story** using a given number of vocabulary words. Give bonus points for each word they can make into a character in the story.

7. Present the students with a list of sentences using the vocabulary words. The students are to tell whether or not a word is **used correctly** in each sentence.

8. **Write riddles** in which the clues tell the meaning of a word and the answer to the riddle is the word. "I'm thinking of a word that means_____."

9. In cooperative groups, have the students use the vocabulary words to prepare either a **crossword puzzle** or a **word search puzzle** which they then present to another group.

10. Locate a **vocabulary word**. Divide the class into teams. Have each team look in the book to find a given word in a section for one point, two points if the group can give the definition of the word, and three points if they can use the word in a sentence.

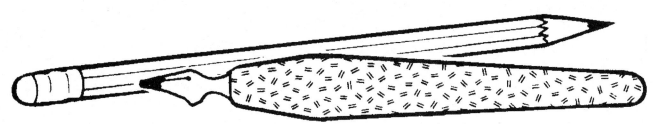

Quiz Section 1

1. On the back of this paper, write a paragraph to describe three important events from Section 1. Then, complete the rest of the questions on this page.

2. Why does Anne decide to name her diary "Kitty"?

   _____

   _____

3. How were Jews made to suffer after Germany invaded Holland?

   _____

   _____

   _____

4. Who in Anne's life died shortly before Anne began her diary, and how did that affect Anne?

   _____

5. What does Anne think about boys?

   _____

6. How does Anne's world "turn up side down" on July 5, 1942?

   _____

   _____

7. What do Anne and her father do immediately to bring order to their new world?

   _____

8. Describe how Anne sees her new home.

   _____

   _____

9. How has the entrance to the Secret Annexe been concealed and by whom?

   _____

   _____

10. On the back of this page, give at least one example of Anne's sense of humor and her way of responding to life.

Make a Time Line of the World's Major Religions

In groups of five or six, each person is to research a religion of the student's choice to learn its basic beliefs and its time and place of origin. Some of the religions you will want to cover include Judaism, Islam, Buddhism, Hinduism, Shinto, and the main branches of Christianity: Roman Catholicism, Eastern Orthodox Christianity, and Protestantism. Just as there are branches of Christianity, there also are branches within each of the other religions, and you may wish to choose one of those branches to research.

Only one person in each group should research each religion. Find the answers to the following questions regarding the religion, or branch of religion, you have chosen:

* Where in the world did this religion begin?

* Where in the world is this religion practiced today?

* Who is the person or persons who are credited with establishing this religion?

* When did this religion begin?

* What are at least five of the basic beliefs of this religion?

After completing your research, come back together in your groups and share what you have learned. Together, try to determine any relationships which exist among the religions your group has researched. For example, there are historic relationships between Judaism, Christianity, and Islam. What are they?

With the information you have obtained, make a time line showing the time relationships of the different religions on a piece of butcher paper or computer paper. Under the heading naming each religion, list the following:

* Time of origin\
* Place of origin
* Founder(s) of this religion

* Where the religion is practiced today
* Basic beliefs

How far back will your time line go? Do you believe that there were any religions before the earliest date on your time line? Why do you believe that?

Anticipation Guide

Your students will enjoy and understand a book better if they prepare for reading it by considering some questions which are pertinent to the book, its setting, and its story. This is particularly true when the book is as powerful and as thought-provoking as the diary of Anne Frank.

Before the students begin reading the book, show it to them and explain that before they read it, they are to thoughtfully give their opinions in response to some statements. Tell them that there are no right or wrong answers and that they will not be graded on their answers.

After students have completed the Anticipation Guide, discuss their answers and the reasons they answered the way they did. After the reading of the book is completed, give these same statements to the students again. Have their opinions changed in any way? If so, how? Return both guides to the students and have them compare their answers both before and after reading the book.

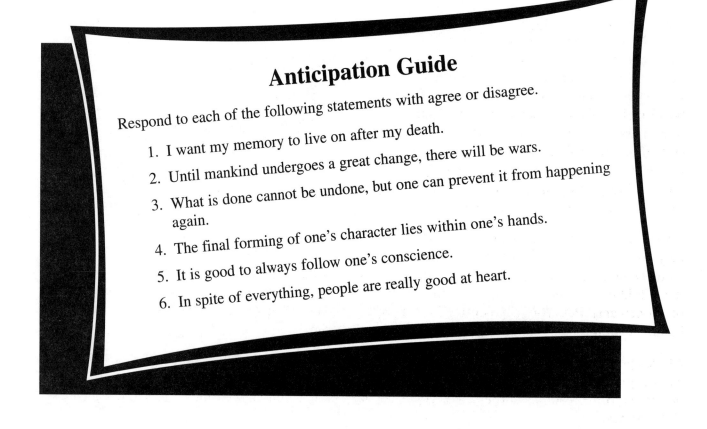

Anticipation Guide

Respond to each of the following statements with agree or disagree.

1. I want my memory to live on after my death.
2. Until mankind undergoes a great change, there will be wars.
3. What is done cannot be undone, but one can prevent it from happening again.
4. The final forming of one's character lies within one's hands.
5. It is good to always follow one's conscience.
6. In spite of everything, people are really good at heart.

Judaism: Anne Frank's Religion

Anne Frank and her family, along with six million other people in Europe, were sent to their deaths for one reason: they were Jewish. They had not broken laws, hurt people with their beliefs, or done anything wrong, but the Nazi German government of the time considered them guilty of the greatest crime of all: having been born members of a certain religion called Judaism.

Judaism is the oldest living religion in the world and presently claims over fourteen million members. Historically, it was the first religion to teach **monotheism,** a belief in one God, rather than belief in many gods as older religions taught. The **Jews,** as modern members of Judaism are called, believe that God entered into a special covenant with the ancient **Israelites,** the early Jews, and that they were chosen by God.

Judaism stresses the importance of behaving in certain ways, rather than strictly believing certain doctrines. There are many different groups of Jews whose beliefs differ in many ways from each other, but probably the central belief to which all Jews hold is that people should treat others as they, themselves, wish to be treated. In Christianity, this same belief is called the **Golden Rule.**

The basic book containing Jewish beliefs is the Hebrew Bible, especially the first five books called the **Torah,** or the **Pentateuch.** Jewish tradition says God revealed his laws to humanity within these books. Other writings of Jewish belief include the Mishnah, the Talmud, and the Jewish prayer book. Judaism also includes a system of laws called the **Halachah** which regulates civil and criminal justice, family relationships, ethics and manners, social responsibilities, and religious observances.

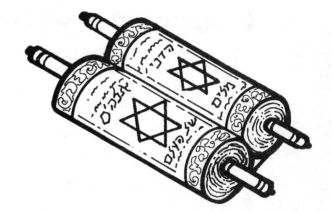

Jews observe the Sabbath, which lasts each week from sunset Friday to sunset Saturday. On this day they do not work, and the ladies of the household light candles. Jews maintaining traditional ways recite certain prayers over a glass of wine and attend synagogue services. Parents say blessings over their children. Traditional religious holidays include **Rosh Hashanah** (New Year), **Yom Kippur** (Day of Atonement), **Passover, Shavuoth** (Feast of Weeks), and the **Feast of Tabernacles.** Other holidays include **Chanukah** (pronounced HAH-nuh-kuh) and **Purim.**

At the age of thirteen a Jewish boy is considered old enough to take on adult religious responsibilities, and he goes through a rite of passage called a **Bar Mitzvah.** His new status is marked by his taking part in the Bible readings during a synagogue service. Girls go through a similar ceremony called a **Bat Mitzvah.**

For centuries, Jewish people have been persecuted for their beliefs in many ways, by prejudice, discriminatory laws, expulsion, and in Nazi Germany, extermination. In ancient Rome Jews could not become citizens. Early Christians believed the Jews were responsible for the death of Christ, and they used this to justify their persecution.

Judaism: Anne Frank's Religion *(cont.)*

Between the thirteenth and fifteenth centuries Jews in Spain were persecuted under the Inquisition, a movement led by the Roman Catholic Church which tortured and killed Jews who would not become Christians. In the fifteenth century, Jews were expelled from the country. In many countries, Jews were forced to live in **ghettos,** walled areas to which the Jews were confined separately from non-Jews (Gentiles). Within ghettos Jews maintained their own businesses, schools, and professions. All the kinds of discrimination against Jews are called **anti-Semitism.**

During the Crusades, from 1096 to 1348, many Jews fled to eastern Europe to be safe. At first they were left alone, but a rumor was started that Jews had poisoned the wells, and persecutions began there, too. When Poland was divided in 1772, 1793, and 1795, masses of Jews suddenly found themselves in Russia, where they underwent severe government attacks called **"pogroms."** One result of the pogroms was that many Jews emigrated from East Europe to the United States, where they were granted religious freedom. During the late 18th century and the French Revolution, a belief in the separation of church and state led many countries to grant Jews equal status, citizenship, and religious freedom.

When Hitler became the dictator of Germany, anti-Semitism and hatred of anything Jewish became official government policy. This was accomplished largely by the use of propaganda, in which the government systematically manipulated the beliefs, attitudes, and actions of the German people. His Minister of Propaganda was a fanatical anti-Semite named Joseph Goebbels, who was able to control all of the press, radio, film, theater, literature, and art produced first in Germany and then in all the other countries conquered by Germany. No part of the media or the arts could escape his control, so the people in Nazi-held countries heard only one side of any question, the official Nazi side, which was anti-Semitic.

The Jews were made scapegoats for their religion; that is, they were blamed by the government for all the troubles Germany had after their defeat in World War I. Their beloved symbol, the Star of David, which is a six-pointed star, was used as a mark which they had to wear on the outside of their clothing to easily identify them so they could be discriminated against more readily. In every aspect of life, Jews were shown to be dirty, evil, dishonest, ugly, and less than human. They were forbidden to mingle in any way with other people, and they were murdered by the millions by the government.

This is the atmosphere into which Anne Frank, her family, and all other European Jews were thrown.

Complete the activity on page 15 to better understand how the Nazi government was able to promote its policy of prejudice and discrimination.

Propaganda and Advertisement

Hitler controlled the countries he conquered by an intensive use of propaganda. He used symbols such as words, gestures, slogans, flags, and uniforms to stand for the people he said were superior to others. He allowed only one side of any opinion. He used different forms of propaganda, including simple persuasion to forms as extreme as psychological warfare and brainwashing.

Modern advertising is also a form of propaganda, because an advertiser wants the consumer audience to believe only one side of an opinion about a product and then buy it.

An advertiser does market research to find out what the consumer thinks and believes about certain products, the most appealing packaging of products, and consumer response to different sales and advertising techniques. This information is then used to mount one-sided advertising campaigns which promise to increase sales.

One way in which advertising campaigns try to appeal to a large number of people is by making emotional appeals. Fear is the most common form of emotional appeal and is often used to motivate a lot of people to carry out preventive measures. A toothpaste commercial might appeal to people's fear of tooth decay to increase sales. A cigarette poster or billboard might appeal to young persons' fear of not being popular by suggesting that smoking will help them make friends.

Advertisers also use symbols or logos which will be recognized easily by the consumer. Most automobile manufacturers have symbols which they put on their automobiles so that people will easily recognize them as standing for quality or luxury. Food companies have symbols such as the fat little "doughboy" used by one or a running athlete used by another.

Do the following:

1. Go to your local grocery store and study the food shelves. List the names of at least 20 products which contain on the package any of these:

    a recognizable logo or symbol

    an appealing picture of the product inside

    any statement which suggests this product is the only good one

2. Watch one hour of television and record the following about each commercial you see:

    Does this commercial appeal to fear?

    Does this commercial use a symbol or logo which stands for the product being advertised?

    Does this commercial say a rival product is bad or not nearly as good?

    Does this commercial suggest that you will be happier or healthier if you use this product?

3. Write a paragraph telling how this activity makes you how you feel about advertising. Does it cahange how you feel?

Reading Response Journals

Competent readers relate personally to what they read. They empathize with a story's characters and can imagine themselves in similar situations. They contribute meaning to each story they read, even as they take meaning from it. Teaching your students new ways to relate to what they read can help them better understand and enjoy the book.

Reading response journals can enable your students to enrich their reading experience by giving their reading structure and form. In these journals, students can be encouraged to respond in a variety of ways to their reading. Try some of these ideas with your students.

- Tell your students the purpose of the journals is to allow them to record their thoughts, observations, questions, and ideas as they read the book.

- Before students read a section or subsection, give them specific questions to consider as they read the section.

- Have students use their journals to take notes on cultural or historical background that you provide to help them better understand the context of the book.

- Use a variety of reading strategies. Oral reading can be alternated with silent reading, or they can follow along as you read. Allow students to freely ask questions or make pertinent comments about the content of the story. Point out literary terms or examples of literary techniques in the book and have students record them in the journals.

- Record interesting new vocabulary in the journals, along with the definitions. This helps keep the words and their meanings at the front of the students' minds and gives them another forum for using the words in sentences.

- Sometimes, instead of questions for them to answer in their journals, give students an unfinished sentence to complete as the beginning of a piece of writing. Always try to provide sentence beginnings or questions which ask the students to really think about what they write.

- Assure the students that although you may respond in writing to what they say in their journals, the journals are their private journals and will not be read aloud in class without their permission.

- Write in journals daily. If possible, keep them in a special place in the classroom. This helps prevent the journals from being damaged on the school grounds and tells the students they are important for their learning.

- Make a concerted effort to keep the use of the journals a positive experience.

Quiz Section 2

1. On the back of this paper, write a paragraph describing three important events from section two. Then complete the rest of the questions on this page.

2. The "honeymoon period" in which the two families get along well does not last very long. Describe some of ways in which they begin to show their differences.

   _____

   _____

   _____

3. How are Anne and her mother not getting along with each other?

   _____

4. What are some of the problems of going into hiding?

   _____

   _____

5. Why is Anne depressed by the news Elli brings her from the "outside"?

   _____

   _____

6. How does Anne see her parents differently?

   _____

   _____

7. Who is the newest inhabitant of the Secret Annexe, and how does he affect Anne?

   _____

   _____

8. Relate the story of Mrs. Van Daan and the dentist.

   _____

   _____

9. How are the people of the Secret Annexe frightened and why?

   _____

10. On the back of this page, discuss the many adjustments Anne has to undergo in the Secret Annexe.

Draw Anne's Room

Read Anne's description of her tiny room and study the floor plan of it below to determine how it is after Dussel moves into it. When looking at the plan of the building in the book, remember that what Americans call the "first floor" is called the "ground floor" in Europe, so the first floor in the plan would actually be considered the second floor by most Americans, and Anne's room was be on the third floor. The bottom, or ground floor, in the building was a warehouse and showroom, and its floor plan is not included in the book's illustration.

After you have carefully studied the floor plan and read Anne's description of her room, draw a picture of it the way you see it in your mind. A floor plan of Anne's room and the Frank's bed-sitting room is below. Draw "walls" out from the floor plan of Anne's room and decorate them as she did.

Remember that "blackout" was in operation at all times. Dark curtains covered all windows to keep light from being seen from the outside when the inhabitants had lights on, and windows were additionally covered with the lace curtains so loved by Europeans which give privacy from the street. What other things does Anne mention in her room?

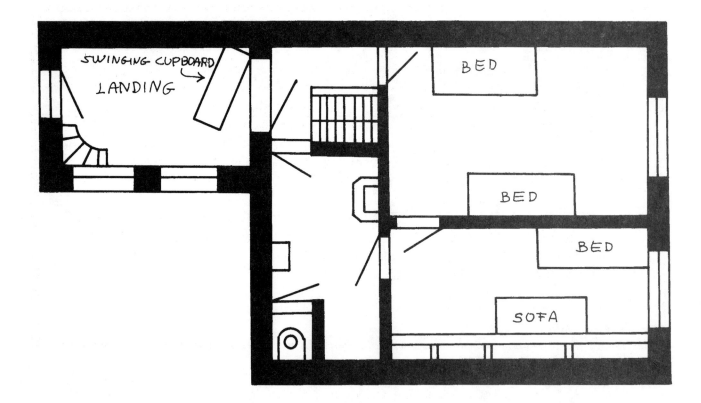

Being in Hiding

For over two years Anne and seven other people were in hiding. There were many ways in which this was a dangerous thing to do but less dangerous than being caught would have been. Since the building housed a business which was operating during the week, and since strangers who knew nothing about them were apt to come into the business at anytime, the inhabitants of the Secret Annexe had to be very quiet during the day. There was a standing reward given for anyone who turned in people in hiding, and very few people, even other Jews, were privy to the fact that the Franks were still in Amsterdam or that they were hidden away in an attic apartment.

Being quiet meant no coughing, talking, laughing, playing a radio, moving about the attic, running water, or flushing the toilet. The inhabitants went to elaborate lengths to ensure that no one below would hear a single sound from above. Over the two years of hiding, there were several scary times: when burglars entered the business below when the property was sold without their knowledge and the new owner came wanting to see his newly acquired building and when neighbors shined a flashlight into the building because they heard a noise. During these times, Anne, her family, and the others cringed in fear, dreading the worst.

Activity: In this activity, you are to pretend that you are an inhabitant of the Secret Annexe, hiding from the Gestapo. SS officers have come into the business showroom below, and you must remain absolutely silent as long as they are in the building. At a signal from the teacher no one in the classroom may make a sound. Any urge to cough, laugh, talk, or make any noise whatsoever must be stifled. You are to maintain this silence until the teacher gives the signal that the silence has ended. Remember, everyone in the classroom is in this together.

When the silence is over, discuss with other students their reactions—how they felt, what went through their minds when they were unable to make a sound, how Anne must have yearned for conversation at the ages of thirteen and fourteen, only to have to remain silent every day for over two years.

To the teacher: This activity can be an extremely powerful experience for the students. Careful preparation is necessary, and the students must understand that this is an opportunity for them to develop their ability to control their behavior in a way which was imperative for many, many people who went into voluntary exile during the war. Some of the students who have the most trouble controlling their behavior in ordinary situations may get really caught up in this activity and may wish to try the activity again to determine whether they can improve their ability to "hide out" from the Gestapo.

A Short History of Nazi Germany

In 1900, Germany, a very large country compared to most of its tiny European neighbors, was Europe's strongest power. When it was defeated by a combination of allies, including England, France, Italy, and the United States, in World War I, it proclaimed itself a republic and sued for peace. The German leaders hoped to help frame the Treaty of Versailles which ended the war, but all the victorious Allies except the United States were determined to punish the new republic.

The Allies forced Germany to sign the Treaty of Versailles, inflicting huge penalties on the beaten country. The treaty placed full blame for the war on Germany and stripped it of its territories. Germany was disarmed and ordered to pay huge amounts for the damages it had done to civilian properties in all of Europe. The punishment was more than most Germans would accept. Not only were they impoverished by the terms of the treaty, but the proud people were severely humiliated.

The anger and indignation the German people felt did not lessen as time went on, and the economic results of the treaty included upwardly spiraling inflation, taking much of what they needed for their daily needs. Most Germans did not accept blame for the war and felt they were being unfairly singled out as the cause of a war which had multiple causes. The feeling their country had been "stabbed in the back" grew through the 1920s and gave rise to various nationalistic groups. One of these groups, the National Socialist German Worker's Party, led by a former house painter named Adolf Hitler, grew as it attracted all sorts of malcontents. They called themselves Nazis.

Hitler's entire life and personality were governed by hate and anger. A gifted orator, he was able to arouse the enthusiasm of huge groups of people. Hitler's message to the German people was that the Jews had caused all of Germany's woes and that they were at fault for Germany's decline in world prestige. He said that "real" Germans were the members of a superior Aryan race and that the Jews, Gypsies, and the Slavs of Eastern Europe were subhuman, not fit to live in civilized society.

Hitler touched an old racist nerve in the German masses as he preached his message of violence and hate, and the racism he encouraged fed on the humiliations of the postwar years. The German people longed to once again have their former power and prestige, and Hitler's party attracted a wide following.

The Nazi Party was one of many small political parties in Germany. In 1932, thirteen years after it began, the Nazis became the largest party in the Reichstag, Germany's legislative body. The aged President von Hindenburg of the Republic was unable to keep control, and in 1933 Hitler convinced the old man to appoint him Chancellor of Germany. Immediately, Hitler demanded that the Reichstag grant him emergency powers for four years. The Reichstag gave in to Hitler's demands and then dissolved itself. Hitler, within two months of becoming Chancellor, became absolute ruler of Germany.

A Short History of Nazi Germany *(cont.)*

From then on, nothing could stop him. Before he committed suicide twelve years later, fifty-five million people would die in Europe.

Many people did not believe that Hitler would eliminate all those he considered unworthy to live, but most German people accepted his rule. Those who did not turned their heads and closed their eyes as he developed his dreaded secret police, the Gestapo, turned his Storm Troopers loose on Jews, and began the grisly job of erecting places of mass murder and slave labor, the concentration camps. A few Jews left Germany during the early years, but escape soon became impossible for most.

Hitler moved quickly to put his racist theories into practice. Jews were dismissed from government positions and forbidden to work in universities, schools, radio, movies, the theater, or journalism. They were not allowed to practice law or medicine or engage in business. All their means of earning a livelihood were taken from them. Jews were segregated, and Jewish children were forbidden to go to school with non-Jewish children. Non-Jews could not work for Jews or marry them.

In 1939 the army Hitler had been preparing for six years began to roll. Poland fell in eighteen days to Germany. Denmark, Norway, Holland, Belgium, and France were conquered within six months. Hitler had signed a non-aggression treaty with Joseph Stalin, the dictator of the Soviet Union, but it did not stop him from attacking that country, as well. A dark cloud had descended on Europe. For the six years it took the combined forces of England, the United States, Russia, and the underground forces to liberate Europe, Hitler's concentration camps continued as efficient killing machines, and all Europe was devastated. Total evil had been turned on the continent of Europe, an evil that would not be defeated until May, 1945.

Activity: Could Hitler have been stopped?

One of the great questions of the twentieth century is whether or not Hitler could have come into power under different political, social, or economic climates than the ones which did exist. Choose one of the following, and write a page discussing the statement: Hitler could not have come into power if. . .

1. the German economy had been healthy and strong.

2. the Allies had allowed Germany to participate in the peace talks of 1919 and not punished the country so severely.

3. Germany would have had two strong democratic political parties.

4. President Hindenburg had said no to Hitler's demands.

5. the Reichstag had said no to Hitler's demands.

6. there had been widespread public demonstrations against Hitler's policies.

7. children had been taught in school the dangers of anti-Semitism.

In your paper give specific reasons why you believe your opinion would have been true and how that situation would have prevented the terrible consequences of Hitler's reign of terror. Also answer the question: **Could what happened in Germany happen again there or anywhere else?**

Write a Letter to Anne

Adolescence is often a difficult time of life for many young people. They are just beginning to learn how to use their suddenly large bodies, and they are trying to find ways to assert their new desire for greater independence. In a matter of a few years, they have gone from being young children to being close to adulthood. While this is exciting and gives a new sense of having personal power, it is also a little frightening, because there is sometimes a little fear of what will come next.

Think about your own adolescence. How do you feel? How do you respond to others, especially adults? What do you want to do with your life? Next, think about Anne's adolescence having to be spent in a tiny attic apartment hidden away from all the fun and friends which she had every right to expect and living with people she doesn't always like very much. Below, write a letter to her explaining how you empathize with her and want to help her. Give her your best advice as a friend on how she can best deal with the daily problems she now faces.

Date _____

Dear Anne,

_____

_____

_____

_____

_____

_____

_____

Sincerely,

_____

Quiz Section 3

1. On the back of this page, write a paragraph describing three important events from Section 3 and then answer the rest of the questions on this page.

2. What does Anne witness through the window in the attic?

   _____

3. How do eighty percent of Dutch students reply to German demands that they sign a loyalty oath to Germany, and with what result?

   _____

   _____

4. Why does Anne ask Dussel for time at the table?

   _____

5. In what daily way is the war on the outside affecting Anne and her family?

   _____

   _____

6. How does Anne spend her days?

   _____

   _____

7. Why does Anne think it is better to talk to herself than to others at the dinner table?

   _____

   _____

8. How does Peter get the bread which Elli forgets to bring upstairs?

   _____

9. What does Anne say will do her more good than 10 Valerian pills?

   _____

10. On the back of this page, describe the daily lives of the inhabitants in the Secret Annexe.

Greek and Roman Mythology

Anne spent a lot of her study time reading Greek and Roman mythology. It was her favorite subject, although the others in the Secret Annexe thought it a little strange that a girl her age should be so fascinated with mythology. People have been reading and telling stories from the mythology of ancient Greece for over two thousand years, so Anne really was not all that strange for liking it.

Greek mythology includes stories about all of the gods and goddesses in which the Ancient Greeks believed. There were twelve altogether. Their names follow:

Zeus (Father of the Gods)	Hephaestus	Hermes
Hera	Demeter	Artemis
Athena	Ares	Poseidon
Aphrodite	Apollo	Dionysus

Choose one of the Greek gods or goddesses. In the library or from a book at home, read the story of the god or goddess you have chosen. When you know the story well, make a papier-mâché mask in the image which you think resembles that god or goddess. Using your mask as a prop, tell the story of the god or goddess to the rest of the class.

To make a papier mâché mask you will need: large bowl, cooking oil, mixing bowl for paste, large spoon or stick for stirring the paste, strips of newspaper or paper towels, wallpaper paste, objects for forming features (examples: paper cups, thread spools, egg-carton cups, toilet-tissue spools, pieces of cardboard), tempera paint, paintbrush

Directions:

1. Carefully mix the wallpaper paste with water according to the directions on the package.

2. Turn the bowl upside down. Grease the bottom with cooking oil.

3. Use paste to apply two layers of newspaper or paper towel strips to the bottom of the bowl.

4. Add features, such as a nose, eyes, ears, and mouth, using a variety of objects and pieces of cardboard.

5. Cover the features with additional layers of paper strips and paste.

6. Let your mask dry thoroughly and then remove the bowl.

7. When the mask is completely dry, paint it.

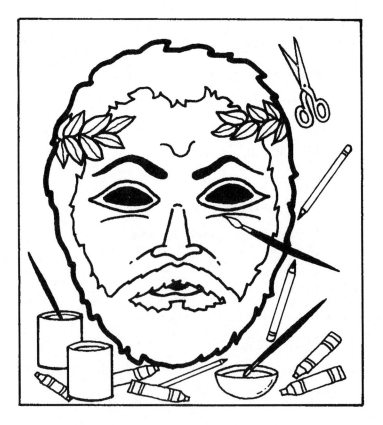

Radio Journalism

A newscast is a telling, or reading, of the news on radio or television. The news is anything important which has happened that day. During World War II there was no television as we have now, and people got much of their news and entertainment from radio. Radio was especially important for the people in the Secret Annexe, because except for the news brought to them by the people who were sheltering them, they were isolated; yet, their lives depended on how the war progressed. It is easy to picture them sitting anxiously around their contraband radio each day.

The professions of writing, producing, and editing the news for radio or television broadcasting is a form of journalism, and the people who do it are called journalists. Many of the rules observed by newspaper journalists are also observed by broadcast media journalists. The broadcaster must tell the who, what, where, when, and how or why of an event. The broadcaster is also expected to tell the truth without prejudice.

In groups of five or six, prepare a radio newscast such as the one the Franks might have heard on their illegal radio. Research a certain incident during the war, such as the invasion of Europe by the allied forces, called D-Day, or the day the Germans surrendered, called Victory in Europe or VE Day, and then write a radio script telling the news as a radio newscaster would tell it. Listen to the news on radio and television now and use the people telling the news as models for your own broadcast. Write and prepare your news carefully. Do the following:

1. **Decide the event you want to cover.**

2. **Write the newscast.**

   Tell who made the news.

   Tell what the person or group did.

   Tell where it was done.

   Tell when it was done.

   Tell how or why it happened.

   Then, fill in the details in a script which the anchor will follow.

3. **Choose the editor,** one person to double-check the accuracy and clarity of the script.

4. **Choose your anchor or anchors,** one person or a pair of persons, to read or tell the news.

5. **Choose the director,** one person to give the anchors directions.

6. **Read or tell the news** on your script into a tape recorder and then play your "broadcast" to the rest of the class.

The Holocaust

The word **holocaust** means total destruction, usually by fire. Since World War II it has earned a new meaning: the massacre of six million Jews by the German Nazis. Hitler's main goal was to exterminate all the Jews in Europe, and he succeeded in killing two-thirds of them before he ended his own life with poison in his bunker under the German Chancellery building in Berlin.

The Holocaust began as soon as Hitler took power. Between 1933 and 1939 the Nazis boycotted Jewish businesses, established quotas in the professions and schools, outlawed marriages between Jews and Gentiles, and built Dachau, Buchenwald, and Oranienburg, the first concentration camps. On the night of November 9, 1938, Hitler's Storm Troopers went on a rampage, burning 267 synagogues, arresting 20,000 people, and smashing Jewish places of business in an orgy of terror which has since been called **Kristallnacht,** "the night of broken glass." To make a horrible night worse, the Nazis then forced the Jews to pay an "atonement" fine of $400 million for the damage which had been done by the government to the Jews' own property.

World War II began for Europe in September, 1939. (The United States did not enter the war until December, 1941.) After Germany conquered Poland, Reinhard Heydrich decreed that all Polish Jews were to be confined in a **ghetto.** Seven hundred thousand of them died during the next two years, and when Germany attacked the Soviet Union in June 1941, "strike squads" were sent in against Soviet Jewish citizens. In one atrocity alone, 33,771 Jews were machine-gunned on September 29, 1941.

In January, 1942 Hitler called the **Wannsee Conference** to debate what he called the "final solution of the Jewish question." As a result, during the next three years Jews represented over half of those exterminated in the concentration camps. Gypsies, Slavs, and political prisoners made up most of the rest. Several camps, including **Auschwitz,** were actually extermination camps built to kill people. The Nazis were proud of their efficiency in murder, and their methods included cyanide or carbon monoxide gas, electrocution, and phenol injections.

The concentration camps have come to stand for the worst that humans can do. They totally debased and depersonalized their inmates, treating them as though they were not people at all, crowding them onto cattle cars, as many as a hundred to a car, and carrying them to the camps without water, food, or sanitary facilities. They abused them physically and verbally in the worst ways possible and split up families, sending men and boys to one place and women and girls to another. In **Auschwitz** the infamous medical director, Dr. Mengele, decided with one look at the incoming prisoners which ones would live and which would die.

Everything they owned—money, clothing, books, jewelry, even the hair on their heads and the gold fillings in their teeth—was taken from them. They slept on wooden shelves which served as beds, crowded so closely together they could not turn over in their sleep, without blankets or pillows.

The Holocaust *(cont.)*

They were forced to work as slave laborers until they could no longer work and then they were killed. They were called by the numbers tattooed on their arms. Hundreds of thousands died of typhus or other terrible diseases which flourish when people are forced to live together in unsanitary conditions. Thousands of whole families were wiped out.

Having no weapons and weakened by disease and malnutrition, the Jews were isolated from the Allies with little resource except to hide, as the Franks did for two years. Escape was impossible after the early years. Sixty thousand managed to join up with partisan groups who fiercely resisted the Nazis throughout the war, and uprisings occurred in several of the larger ghettos, including the one in Warsaw, Poland.

Those killed included men, women, children, babies, old people, and the handicapped. They included doctors, teachers, librarians, lawyers, business people, store clerks, housewives, students, farmers, and secretaries. People from every walk of life were killed, regardless of who they were, how wealthy or how poor they were or how good or how bad they were. They were all the same to the misfits and criminals who ran the government and the camps.

The camp to which Anne, her mother, and her sister were taken first was Auschwitz in Poland, the largest of the camps and considered a model extermination camp. Its gas chambers were large enough to kill hundreds of people at once and its huge furnaces burned the bodies of the dead. Columns of black smoke rose from the furnaces into the air twenty-four hours a day. Anne's mother died there, then Anne and Margot were taken to **Bergen-Belsen.** In Auschwitz there was a little food to eat, but in Belsen there was nothing. It was only a matter of time until Margot, and then Anne, died of typhus.

The holocaust is one of the darkest chapters in all of human history. It was truly a time when the inmates ran the show, when evil was turned loose on the inhabitants of a whole continent and became official policy.

Activity: In Berlin, once again the capital of Germany, a large monument in memory of the victims of the Holocaust is going to be built over or near Hitler's bunker, which still exists underground. All the known names of the victims will be on the monument.

Design a monument to the victims of the Holocaust. Draw a picture of how it will look and indicate on your plan the following:

What material or materials will you use?

How large will it be?

What symbols will you include, and how will you include them?

How will you landscape the grounds around your monument?

When your monument is finished, what kind of ceremony will you have to dedicate it?

Where will your monument stand?

Prepare an Escape Bag

Anne prepares an "escape bag," because she is terrified that one day they will have to run for their lives from the Secret Annexe. Bombings and gunshots are heard almost daily. She sees people being led down the street by the Gestapo. They listen to the radio news, in itself a crime, and they know now that freedom is not going to come immediately, although they cling to the hope the Allies will defeat Germany.

Anne admits to Kitty that she clings to her escape bag more because she wants something to hold onto than thinking that they have any hope of escaping. As she says, there is nowhere for them to go. Still, it gives her a certain amount of comfort, so it would hold some of her most precious things.

In a tote bag or a large shopping bag, prepare the escape bag you think Anne would have prepared. Inside the bag, place the things, or pictures of things, you believe Anne would take with her if she was forced to flee the Secret Annexe. You know her well enough by this time to know what is dear to her and what is not.

Would she take clothing? _____ If so, what kind? _____

_____

Would she take books? _____ If so, which ones?_____

_____

What decorative items in her tiny room would she take?_____

_____

Would she take any souvenirs of the Secret Annexe?_____

_____

Would she take anything belonging to anyone else? _____ If so, what? _____

_____

Would she take food?_____ If so, what kind? _____

_____

Would she decorate her escape bag? _____ If so, how?_____

_____

Bring your escape bag to share with your classmates. Tell them the reasons you have put into your bag each item you have put there and why each would have been important to Anne.

Extension: Pretend that you are in a dangerous situation similar to Anne Frank's. Prepare an escape bag containing some of your own things that are most precious to you. Share your bag with the class if you would like to.

Quiz Section 4

1. On the back of this paper, write a paragraph describing three important events from Section 4. Then, complete the rest of the questions on this page.

2. Why does hearing about Mrs. Koophius' daughter, Corry, make Anne feel bad?

   _____

3. How is Anne's attitude toward her mother changing as she gets older?

   _____

4. What does Anne make for herself to wear?

   _____

5. What is an abiding interest of Anne's, and how does it cause her to change her appearance from time to time?

   _____

   _____

6. What does Anne mean when she says, "Invasion fever is mounting daily"?

   _____

   _____

7. How has Anne's relationship with Peter changed?

   _____

8. Why does Anne think nature is the best cure for loneliness, and do you agree?

   _____

   _____

9. Instead of thinking about all the misery in the world, what does Anne think about?

   _____

   _____

10. There are many differences in the life Anne lived on the outside and now. What are they, and how does she handle them? Write your answers to this question in a paragraph on the back of this page.

Start a Photo Collection

Anne eagerly collected photographs and movie magazine articles of the movie stars and movies of her time. This was a favorite hobby for many teenaged girls during the 1940s and 1950s, for it was the "Golden Age" of Hollywood. Every movie star had at least one fan club, and any girl who sent off a letter to her favorite star was sure to receive in the mail a signed photo of the star. It probably had been signed by someone working in the studio rather than the star, but the photos were treasured, nonetheless.

Anne looked forward to each new issue of her favorite movie magazines, for within their pages she was able to read about the stars' troubles and see pictures of their home lives, their new films, who was married and who was not, who went to grand movie premieres with whom, and all the latest gossip. She plastered the pictures she took from the magazines all over her room, and she took great pleasure in them.

Activity

Start a photo collection of your own, made up of any photos of your choice: pictures of film stars; pictures of sport stars; pictures of scenery, of animals, or of anything else that you like.

Directions:

1. On a large piece of tagboard or cardboard, arrange a group of your pictures into a collage. Put your pictures into groups based on how they go together in some way, for example, by color or by subject.

2. Put a caption under each picture, telling who or what is in the photo.

3. Use colored tape or wrapping paper to frame your collage.

Bring your collage to school to share with your classmates. Tell why you have chosen to collect the pictures you have and display your collage on the classroom wall.

Writing Proverbs

Although she did not call them proverbs, Anne was continually writing proverbs of her own which revealed the attitudes that were important in her life. A **proverb** is a short saying which expresses a truth or a fact. The Old Testament includes one book which is nothing except proverbs; indeed, its title is The Book of Proverbs.

Some of the proverbs with which Anne filled her diary are the following:

Paper is patient.

I must not bury my head in the blankets, but keep my head high.

Nature bring solace in all troubles.

He who has courage and faith will never perish in misery.

It is better for hard words to be on paper, than that Mummy carry them in her heart.

A friend can't take a mother's place.

Time heals all wounds.

What is going to happen, will happen.

Activities with Proverbs

Good sources of proverbs are The Book of Proverbs, in the *Bible,* and *Bartlett's Familiar Quotations,* which you can probably find in the public library or your school library. In Shakespeare's *Hamlet,* Polonious speaks in proverbs, especially in the speech he gives his son Laertes in Act I, scene iii. *Poor Richard's Almanac* by Benjamin Franklin, if you can find it, is another good source.

1. In groups of three or four, list all the proverbs you can think of or find. Then, compare them with those above and others that Anne wrote in her diary.

   How are the two lists alike? How are they different? What can you tell about Anne's character and personality by the proverbs she keeps?

2. After you have compared the two lists of proverbs, list all the personality traits of Anne's which you can see in the proverbs above and any others you can find in her diary.

3. Choose one of the proverbs you have collected which you like and illustrate it, writing the proverb as a caption under your picture.

Write a News Story

Many people depend on their daily newspapers and certain magazines for news even though they may also watch the television news or listen to radio news broadcasts. The profession of writing, producing, editing, and publishing the news is called journalism. People who do the writing, producing, editing, and publishing the news about current events for newspapers and magazines are called **journalists.**

There are several different kinds of writing which go into a newspaper. **Feature writing** includes wedding announcements, food sections, obituaries, comics, entertainment news, and puzzles. **Sports writing** includes all the news about the various sports and the people involved in them. **Classified writing** includes classified advertising. **Editorial writing** includes writing opinions about current events and the writing of special-interest columns. **News writing** is the writing of general interest news about things which concern a large number of people, such as disasters and political events.

When writing a news story, certain elements of the story must be told very early in the article, usually within the first paragraph. These elements are **who** the story is about, **what** the event was the person or group was involved in, **when** the event happened, **where** it happened, and **how** or **why** it happened as it did. The rest of the article is concerned with relating the details of the story.

An example of a first paragraph for a story about the opening of a new shopping mall might read:

> Russel Carns, president of Dorset's Department Stores, cut the ribbon to open the
> new Mall of the West in Santa Teresa yesterday as two thousand people looked on.

In this paragraph "Russel Carns" is the **who**, "cut the ribbon to open the new Mall" is the **what**, "Mall of the West in Santa Teresa" is the where, "yesterday" is the **when**, and "as two thousand people looked on" is the **how**.

After this short first paragraph, the article would go on, usually in short paragraphs of one to three sentences each, to give all the rest of the details of the opening of the new mall. In order to write the news well, the journalist tries to write as clearly and briefly as possible, so the reader can get most of what is important about the story within the first few paragraphs. A good news story is not biased; that is, the story is not written in such a way that it promotes a particular opinion or position. Opinions belong on the editorial page. A good news story reports only the facts about what happened.

Write a news story with the following facts: Amsterdam bombed by 350 British planes; Sunday afternoon, March 26, 1944; one-half-million kilos of bombs dropped on Ijmuiden; houses trembled like blades of grass in the wind; 1,200 people injured; many homeless without food; militia called up; fires all over the city.

Heroes and Teachers

Most people have heroes. Some heroes are great statesmen; some heroes are people who have accomplished something important, such as a breakthrough in medicine or the invention of something which improves the quality of life. Other people deserve to be called heroes because of their immense courage in spite of personal danger to themselves, such as a firefighter who saves the lives of people trapped in a burning building.

Some people become heroes because a terrible situation brings out the best in them and causes them to take action, at great peril to themselves. Elli, Miep, and the others who brought food and news to the inhabitants of the Secret Annexe were heroes like this; they risked their own lives to try to save the lives of their friends. The greatest heroes become teachers who teach us the real meaning of courage and who show us that true courage has many dimensions.

Anne Frank could be considered another kind of hero, not because she was fearless or saved a lot of people's lives, but because of something she did just by being herself, a very bright and very vulnerable young girl. She wrote a diary which has touched the lives of millions of people in very important ways and which continues to touch the lives of people more than fifty years after her death. In that diary, she opened herself up so the reader can see every aspect of her personality, and having read it, no one could ever again feel quite the same way about prejudice or discrimination. By doing this, Anne Frank, the schoolgirl, became a powerful and very effective teacher.

Activity:

Step 1: Think of someone who is your hero. Name that person and list below all the qualities which make that person a hero to you.

Step 2: Write a paragraph answering these questions.

Why do you respect these qualities in your hero?

Is your hero someone you know?

Do you try to be like your hero? In what ways?

Does your hero make you want to be better in some way?

If you could tell your hero what there is about that person that inspires you to be a better person, what would you say?

_____

_____

_____

_____

Quiz Section 5

1. On the back of this paper, write a paragraph describing three important events from Section 5. Then, complete the rest of the questions on this page.

2. What are some of the most recent news items Anne has heard on the radio?

   _____

   _____

3. What hobbies and interests has Anne developed since going into hiding?

   _____

   _____

   _____

4. How does the atmosphere in the house become terribly strained by one incident?

   _____

   _____

5. Why is 16 April, 1944, an important day in Anne's life?

   _____

6. When she says, "Now we have found each other," what is Anne talking about?

   _____

   _____

7. Why does Anne think "the little man" is just as guilty as the politicians in fighting wars?

   _____

8. What does Anne consider the worst thing she has ever done in her life?

   _____

9. Anne believes that having a religion is a gift. Why does she believe this?

   _____

10. On the back of this paper, discuss this question: Anne says the final forming of a person's character is up to that person. Do you agree, and why?

Coping with Food Cycles

Toward the end of the war, obtaining food became a real problem for many people, including those in the Secret Annexe. The production of food was a problem because of the bombing. The transportation of food was, likewise, subject to interruption, because roads were being destroyed. There were many other reasons why Anne and her "roommates" would find it difficult to get enough food, such as they had to always rely on others to get food for them. The arrest of the vegetable man made getting fresh produce difficult, because he had realized why Miep and Elli bought so much food and kept quiet, supplying them with what they needed. Ration cards were hard to get, and food could not be easily bought without them. Their ration cards had to be bought on the black market at twice the cost of legal ones.

All of this led to what Anne calls their "food cycles," times when they had a lot of one particular food and no other. This meant they scrambled around, trying to find new recipes for a food which one tired of after eating it day after day. This is not as easy as it sounds.

Choose any two of the foods listed and find as many different ways to prepare those foods as you can. Prepare one of your recipes and bring it to share with classmates. Copy the recipe on to the recipe card below.

Which of these foods are favorites of yours? How would you like to eat only that one food for days on end?

Foods

strawberries	beef stew meat	cheddar cheese
potatoes	popcorn	canned tuna fish
corn	eggplant	macaroni
green beans	eggs	cabbage
tomatoes	bologna	bell peppers
chicken	celery	lettuce

Put Hitler on Trial

In November 1945, historic trials began as twenty-two of Hitler's officers were tried for the war crimes they committed by a court made up of judges and officials of the Allies. The trials were held in Nuremberg, Germany, and since that time, the trials have been called the **Nuremberg Trials.** An American judge presided. Ten of those tried were sentenced to death, three were sentenced to life in prison, and the rest were given lesser sentences. Several of the most important men in control of the Nazi regime escaped punishment either by committing suicide or by fleeing Europe and going to South America, where they changed their names and began new lives.

The **International Law** on which the Nuremberg Trials rested defined war crimes as violations by civilian or military personnel against humanity, violations of the rules of conduct of hostilities, mistreatment of civilians and prisoners of war, and belligerent occupation of enemy territory. Crimes against the peace include **aggression** of one country against another. Crimes against humanity include the crime of **genocide,** which is the killing of whole groups of people, such as the Jews in Germany.

The most important decision of the court at Nuremberg was that no one has the right to violate the rights of another even when ordered to do so by a superior. Several of the Nazis tried at Nuremberg used as their excuse for the crimes they committed that they were only following orders. The court said that no one can use that as an excuse for committing crimes against humanity, that each person is responsible for his or her own conduct.

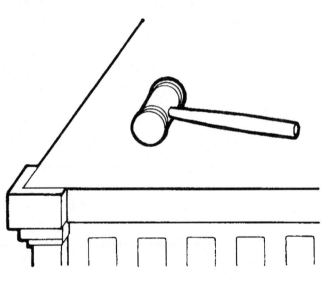

Hitler committed suicide with his mistress, Eva Braun. Goebels, the Minister of Information who was in charge of Nazi propaganda, also committed suicide after killing his wife and six children. Herman Goering, once second only to Hitler himself in power, cheated the hangman's noose by taking poison after he was sentenced to die by hanging.

Most people would agree that each person is responsible for his or her own behavior and that one should not escape punishment for a terrible crime by blaming someone else, or by such excuses as being drunk or on drugs. Yet Hitler, Goebbels, and Goering, rather than face the consequences of their acts, committed suicide. Of the three, only one, Goering, was brought to trial.

Hitler masterminded the evil Nazi regime from beginning to end. He was the one who ordered that the Jews all be exterminated. He put into motion a national killing machine which systematically slaughtered people in huge camps of death and which invaded other countries for his own ambitions for power. Before his suicide, fifty-five million people in Europe were dead, many killed in horrible, inhuman ways. Historic old European cities were in ruins. His was the ultimate responsibility; yet, he escaped having to pay the consequences for his acts.

Put Hitler on Trial *(cont.)*

Activity

You are going to try Adolf Hitler in absentia, that is, without him present. In order to do this, there are several things you must do. Before you begin divide into groups and assign each group member to do some of the research.

1. You must research Hitler and his Nazi regime and learn as much as you can about it. In 1924 Hitler published a book which he wrote while in prison and in which he told exactly what he intended to do to the Jews and to others he considered subhuman. The name of the book is *Mein Kampf,* which means My Struggle. It shows his entire philosophy to be fanatically anti-Semitic, considering his idea of an Aryan race to be superior to all others, and full of incredible hate. You do not have to read this book, but you do need to research the history of Germany, particularly between 1919 when the Treaty of Versailles was signed and the end of World War II in May 1945.

2. Name the following people to take part in the trial; Write their names here.

   judge or panel of judges _____

   prosecutor _____

   defense lawyer _____

   jury _____

3. The charges against Hitler are that he committed crimes against humanity and crimes of war.

   After the prosecutor has presented the case against Hitler and offered evidence to support the case, the defense lawyer is to try to show why Hitler should not be considered guilty of crimes. The jury will then decide Hitler's guilt or innocence, and if he is found guilty, determine what his punishment will be. Using the space below determine if you find Hitler guilty. Write the arguments that helped you reach your decision.

Diphtheria: An Old Scourge

On Wednesday, November 27, 1943, Anne tells us that Elli is confined to her home with diphtheria. Babies are routinely immunized for diphtheria now, usually in one of the first immunizations they get. This particular immunization is called a "DPT" shot, short for diphtheria, pertussis, and tetanus, three diseases which used to cause many illnesses and deaths, particularly in children, before the immunizations were developed by modern medicine. **Pertussis** is the name for what is usually called "whooping cough," and **tetanus** is the name for what is usually called "lockjaw." Very few people ever get these diseases today, because mass immunization has almost eradicated them.

Diphtheria is an infectious disease caused by a bacillus with a very long name: corynebacterium diphtheria. This organism infects the throat and sometimes the nose, skin, or wounds. It produces a toxin, or poison, which circulates in the bloodstream and causes most of the symptoms. The illness begins slowly with a fever, sore throat, and swollen lymph glands in the neck. A thick, white membrane forms on the tonsils and may hinder breathing so badly that an operation called a tracheotomy to open the windpipe must be performed.

The muscles of the heart and the nerves may also be affected, causing heart failure, paralysis, and, sometimes, death. The paralysis may affect the speech, sight, breathing, or walking of the patient. Today it can be treated with antitoxin and penicillin, which were not available years ago.

Most young people today have never experienced these terrible infectious diseases which used to kill thousands of children each year, and it is easy to think they have disappeared and will never come back. It is important to remember that although we do not see them now, the war against them must continue. The immunizations must still be given, for if we get careless and stop immunizing people against the diseases, it will not be long before they rear their ugly heads and start killing children again.

Complete the activity on page 39 to learn more about the immunizations which children or adults might have on the next page.

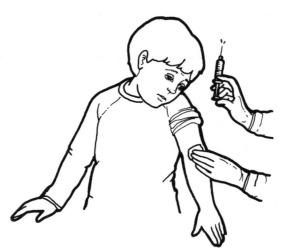

Immunizations

Ask your parents, the school nurse, or your doctor which of these "childhood diseases" is now prevented by immunizations and at what age. Some immunizations must be given more than once. Check the ones which require "booster shots." Check with your parents or your doctor to find out when you were given these shots. Write the date you received the shots in the column below.

Immunization	Age Given	Booster Needed?	My Immunization Record
Diphtheria			
Tetanus			
Whooping cough			
Polio			
Measles (red)			
German measles			
Mumps			
Scarlet fever			
Influenza			
Pneumonia (viral)			
Meningitis (viral)			
Encephalitis			
Chicken pox			

The Final Day in the Secret Annexe

Tuesday, 1 August, 1945, is the last entry in Anne's diary. On or shortly after that day the Franks, the Van Daans, and Dussel were arrested after an anonymous phone call to the police betrayed them. We have short, scattered personal reminiscences of people who saw them in the camps, but other than that, we do not know exactly what happened on that day, except that we know it was bound to be unpleasant.

Imagine that Anne was able to write one day's entry into her diary about what happened before her diary was discarded by those who arrested her. How would she have described her arrest and her first day in custody? What would the arresting officers have said, and what would Anne have replied? Write one last entry in Anne's diary, describing what happened.

Use dialogue in your diary entry, as Anne often did. **Remember the following when writing dialogue:**

- Capitalize the first word in any quotation if it is the beginning of a quoted sentence.

- If the quotation begins in the middle of a quoted sentence, do not capitalize the first word.

- Separate by commas the explanatory words which tell who is talking.

- Enclose punctuation within the quotation marks.

Examples:

capital   period

Anne said, "In spite of everything I still believe that people are really good at heart."

comma

no capital

"In spite of everything I still believe," Anne said, "that people are really good at heart."

commas   period

Any Questions?

When you finish reading a good book, especially one like Anne Frank's, you become very involved with the characters so that when you finish, you still have many questions. What are some of the questions you have after finishing *Anne Frank: The Diary of a Young Girl?* Write them here.

In small groups, or by yourself, try to come up with possible answers for the following questions, as well as the ones you have written above; then, come together as a class and discuss some of your ideas.

_____

_____

_____

_____

_____

- How did the other occupants of the Secret Annexe really feel about Anne? What did Peter look like? Was Mrs. Van Daan really a complainer and whiner as Anne pictured her? Did Anne really feel as bad about her mother as she writes she did, or did she just write about her mother when she was angry?

- Was Anne funny? Was she really fascinated by sexual matters? Did Anne's parents play favorites with the two daughters? What did Peter and Anne really talk about all those times they spent together? What happened to Peter when he was taken by the Germans? If Anne had not died, would she have stayed in love with Peter? Did she really love him, or was the attraction there simply because there were no other boys for her to love?

- What happened to Miep, Elli, Koophius, and all the others who kept them supplied with food and protected them? Were they ever arrested for hiding the Franks? If not, why not? What happened to the vegetable man who suspected they were in hiding and said nothing? Was Dussel really a nice man, or was he petty and pedantic as Anne portrayed him? How much of Anne's criticism of others was due to her being the youngest person in the Secret Annexe?

- Who betrayed the Franks? Did Anne continue being an optimist after she was taken to the concentration camp? Did she and her mother become close before they died? How many lives have been changed by reading Anne's diary?

Research Ideas

Describe three things in *Anne Frank: The Diary of A Young Girl* that you would like to learn more about.

1. _____

2. _____

3. _____

Anne Frank: The Diary of a Young Girl contains many references to people, places, and events. Anne talks about events she has heard about on the radio, books and stories she has read, and places around the world you may never have heard about before. Researching some of the people, places, and events in the book can help you gain a better understanding of the book and a better appreciation of Anne's craft as a writer.

In groups, or on your own, research one or more of these topics listed below. Share what you have discovered with the class in any appropriate format for oral presentation.

Weimar Republic
Holocaust
Berlin
Luftwaffe
Invasion of Europe
Anti-Semitism
Warsaw Ghetto
Victory in Europe
Chanuka
World War II
America in World War II
German occupation of Poland
German occupation of Holland
The USSR-Germany Non-aggression
Pact
U-Boats
Albert Einstein
Food rationing
Winston Churchill
English aircraft
Conference at Malta
Harold MacMillan
Queen Julianna
Royal Air Force
Pogroms
Israel
Old Testament
Synagogue
Diaspora
Christianity

The Torah
Adolf Hitler
Josef Goebbels
Dunkirk
Treaty of Versailles
Racism
Concentration camps
Judaism
Jewish holidays
The Nuremberg Trials
Battle of Britain
German occupation of France
German occupation of Denmark
Fascism
V-2 Rocket
Werner von Braun
German aircraft
The Iron Curtain
Potsdam Conference
Mussolini
Queen Elizabeth II
Parachutes
French Underground
Terezin Ghetto
The United Nations
Jerusalem
Israelists
Zionism
Islam

Create an Anne Frank Museum

In Amsterdam the building the Franks, Van Daans, and Dussel lived in for over two years is now a museum which many thousands of people visit each year. Visiting the museum is a somber experience, because one cannot help but be struck by the horror of what Anne and her family underwent and by the loss to the world of a girl who had such promise. The diary she wrote is the most powerful memorial possible of the person, Anne Frank. She is, indeed, still living after her death through her effect on the world's conscience and as a constant reminder of a horror which must never happen again. She would like that.

Create in your classroom a museum dedicated to Anne Frank. In your museum you can use these suggestions of displays and activities from your classroom work, as well as your own ideas.

Displays

- Time Lines of World's Major Religions
- Drawings of Anne's Room
- Diaries of Eyewitnesses of Nazi Takeover
- Masks of Greek Gods and Goddesses
- Escape Bags with Explanations
- Letters of Advice to Anne
- Photo Collection Collages
- Proverbs
- News Stories
- Papers on Heroes and Heroes as Teachers
- Recipes for Food Cycles
- Final Journal Entries
- Research Papers and Projects
- Book Reports and Projects
- Display of family photos, magazines, and family souvenirs of World War II
- Posters of movies and movie stars of the 1930s and 1940s.

Activities

- Production of Radio Newscast
- Group Discussions about Preventing Another Holocaust
- Oral Reports on Heroes and Heros as Teachers
- Demonstrations of Foods Cycles
- Hitler on Trial
- Oral Presentation of Book Reports
- Role playing of:

  —hiding from the Gestapo

  —a typical day in the Secret Annexe

  —Chanuka in the Secret Annexe

  —residents listening to the news

- Guest speaker
- Playing recordings of popular music of World War II
- Showing of the movie *Anne Frank*

Unit Test

Matching: Match the descriptions of the characters with their names.

1. _____ Anne Frank   A. Mumsie

2. _____ Peter Van Daan   B. Otto Frank

3. _____ Dussel   C. Gave the girls office work to do

4. _____ Adolf Hitler   D. Gave a young girl her first kiss

5. _____ Margot   E. A young girl's secret friend

6. _____ Miep   F. Hated Jews

7. _____ Mrs. Van Daan   G. Didn't speak to the Van Daans for 10 days

8. _____ Mrs. Frank   H. Queen of the kitchen

9. _____ Pim   I. Her diary captured the hearts of the world.

10. _____ Kitty   J. Beautiful and intelligent

11. _____ Kraler   K. Brought strawberries and potatoes

12. _____ Elli   L. Brought film magazines

True or False: Answer true or false in the blanks below.

1. _____ Anne dislikes history and mythology.

2. _____ Mrs. Van Daan liked tiny potatoes.

3. _____ Whatever happened, Anne remained optimistic and cheerful.

4. _____ Mr. Frank played favorites with his daughters.

5. _____ Miep, Henk, Kraler, Elli, and Koophius risked their lives daily for the Franks.

Short Answer: Write a brief response to each question in the blank provided.

1. What did Anne call their hiding place? _____

2. Who got a dentist's instrument stuck in her tooth? _____

3. In what city was the Frank's hiding place? _____

4. Name three hobbies of Anne's. _____

5. How did Anne feel about the Germans? _____

Essay: Respond to the following on the back of this page.

Sometimes it is said that everyone we know is a teacher for us. While you have met Anne Frank only through her diary, you are able to know her more intimately than we usually are able to know a person. With what you know, how has Anne Frank been a teacher to the world? Has she helped you to know others better than you did? What is the most important thing she taught you, and why is it important?

Response

Explain the meanings of these quotations from *Anne Frank: The Diary of a Young Girl.*

Note to the teacher: Choose the appropriate number of quotes to which your students should respond.

Section 1

"The first to greet me was you, possibly the nicest of all."

"It is just as if the whole world had turned upside down, but I am still alive . . ."

"We walked in the pouring rain . . . each with a school satchel and shopping bag filled to the brim with all kinds of things thrown together anyhow."

"I don't feel at home anywhere without my chamber, she declared."

Section 2

"We simply don't get on together these days."

"It was very different when I was young."

"Our many Jewish friends are being taken away by the dozen."

"I'm not so keen that a stranger should use my things, but one must be prepared to make sacrifices for a good cause."

Section 3

"Though youngest here, you are no longer small,

But life is very hard, since one and all

Aspire to be your teacher . . . "

"We had the first warning siren while we were at breakfast.."

"I could write whole chapters about Madame, and . . . perhaps I will someday."

"First, I hear a sound like a fish gasping for breath . . . then with much ado and interchanged with little smacking sounds, the lips are moistened, followed by a lengthy twisting and turning . . . "

Section 4

"The period when I caused Mummy to shed tears is over."

"I looked into his deep blue eyes, and he sat there with that mysterious laugh playing round his lips."

"They'll have to be careful that such impudent tricks do not reach the ears of Germans."

"It is getting more and more wonderful here."

"I don't think then of all the misery, but of the beauty that still remains."

Section 5

"It's really disagreeable to eat a lot of sauerkraut for lunch and supper everyday."

"I want to go on living after my death!"

"The married couple with the torch would probably have warned the police."

"I regard our hiding as a dangerous adventure, romantic and interesting at the same time."

"In spite of everything I still believe that people are really good at heart."

Bibliography of Related Reading

Mythology

D'Aulaire, Ingri, and Edgar P. D'Aulaire. *D'Aulaires' Book of Greek Myths.* Doubleday, 1962

Evslin, Evslin, and Hoopes. *The Greek Gods.* Scholastic, 1966

Harrison, Jane Ellen. *Mythology.* Harcourt, Brace & World, Inc., 1963

Sewell, H. and Thomas Bullfinch. *A Book of Myths.* Macmillan, 1969

Young People During Wartime

Collier, James Lincoln, and Christopher Collier. *My Brother Sam Is Dead* (American Revolution). Scholastic, 1974

Greene, Bette. *Summer of My German Soldier* (World War II). Bantam Books, 1988.

Houston, Jeanne Wakatsuki and James D. *Farewell to Manzanar* (World War II). Bantam Book, 1974.

Hunt, Irene. *Across Five Aprils* (American Civil War). Berkeley Books, 1991.

Reiss, Johanna. *The Upstairs Room* (World War II). Scholastic Inc., 1990.

Seredy, Kate. *The Singing Tree* (World War I). Scholastic Inc., 1992.

Takashima, Shizuye. *A Child in Prison Camp* (World War II). Tundra Bks., 1991

Prejudice and Discrimination

Hinton, S.E. *The Outsiders.* Dell, 1989.

Taylor, Mildred. *Roll of Thunder. Hear My Cry.* Bantam Books, 1976.

Taylor, Theodore. *The Cay.* Avon Books, The Hearst Corporation, 1970.

Yep, Lawrence. *Child of the Owl.* Harper Collins, 1990.

Yep, Lawrence. *Dragonwings.* Scholastic, 1990.

Other

Adler, David A. *The Number on My Grandfather's Arm.* UAHC Press, 1987

Benchley, Nathaniel. *Bright Candles: A Novel of the Danish Resistance.* Harper & Row, 1974

Kimmel, Eric. *Bar Mitzvah: A Jewish Boy's Coming of Age.* Viking, 1995.

Meltzer, Milton. *RESCUE: The Story of How the Gentiles saved Jews in the Holocaust.* Harper & Row, 1988

Stadtler, Bea. *The Holocaust.* Berhman House, Inc., 1974

The Jewish Museum, Prague. *I Have Not Seen a Butterfly Around Here. Children's Drawings and Poems From Terezin,* Prague, 1993.

Answer Key

Quiz Section 1 (page 10)

1. Accept appropriate answers

2. She wants her diary to be her friend.

3. They had to wear a Star of David in plain view, give up their bicycles, were banned from teams (streetcars), were forbidden to drive, allowed to shop only at certain times, could shop only in Jewish shops, had to keep curfew of 8 PM. even in their own gardens, were forbidden to attend movies, theater, and other places of entertainment, could not go to public sports, public pools, public tennis courts, and had to attend Jewish schools, etc.

4. Anne's granny died, and she missed her very much.

5. She likes them, likes to flirt, likes to get attention from them, etc.

6. Her family had to go into hiding.

7. They set about getting things in the Secret Annexe in order.

8. Accept responses which include a physical description of the building.

9. A cupboard was placed over the door to the attic, making it look as though no door was there, by Mr. Vossen.

10. Accept appropriate responses, particularly about when Anne turns punishment into a challenge.

Quiz Section 2 (page 17)

1. Accept appropriate answers.

2. The Van Daan's quarrel; Anne sees Peter as lazy and hypochondriacal; Mrs. Van Daan, petty about everyone using her china, yells at Anne, etc.

3. Anne and her mother are not seeing things the same way; Anne thinks her mother doesn't understand her. Anne favors her father over her mother, thinks her mother favors Margot, etc.

4. Problems included lack of privacy, living so closely together with others, not having accustomed bathtubs, and having no freedom.

5. All the news about Jews being arrested, driven through the streets like trash, and being sent off to terrible fates depresses Anne.

6. She sees her father as good, understanding, calm, always there for her and sees mother as not understanding her, picking on her, favoring her sister over her, always finding fault with little things.

7. Dussel, the dentist, has moved into Anne's room. She has no privacy, and she disagrees with many of Dussel's ideas as to how children should be raised.

8. Mrs. Van Daan complained about a terrible toothache, so Dussel proceeded to examine her mouth. She made such a fuss while he was doing it that the instrument he was using got stuck in her tooth.

9. A burglar was heard in the warehouse; everyone was afraid they had been heard or would be.

10. Accept appropriate responses.

Quiz Section 3 (page 23)

1. Accept appropriate answers.

2. She sees an air fight.

3. They refused to sign and were taken as slave laborers to Germany.

4. He monopolized the only table in their room on which she could do school work so she had no place to do her work.

5. Daily bombings, sounds of shooting, and air raid sirens kept them away.

6. She studies, reads mythology, and does office work for Elli.

7. She won't bore others with her chatter, won't have to be told her opinions are

Answer Key *(cont.)*

stupid, and won't have to listen to opinions of others.

8. He crawls past the office window so no one outside will see him.

9. A good laugh will do her more good.

10. Accept appropriate responses.

Quiz Section 4 (page 29)

1. Accept appropriate answers.

2. It causes her to miss all the things a young girl would normally be able to do—parties, school, etc.

3. She is growing up and beginning to see her mother as another person with feelings and worthy of respect.

4. She makes a ballet skirt.

5. Her love for the photos of film stars and film magazines causes her to change her hair style to that of her film idols.

6. People are talking about little else but the coming invasion.

7. She is beginning to see him as a friend and almost more than that.

8. She longs to be out in the fresh air and nature, believing that nature will cure her of anything.

9. She thinks about good things. If she has to eat something she doesn't like, she imagines that it is something else which she does like. She looks on the bright side of things.

10. Accept appropriate answers.

Quiz Section 5 (page 34)

1. Accept appropriate answers.

2. She has heard about the invasion, about different places which have been taken back from the Germans, especially in France and on the Russian front; also, she

has heard many Christians now blaming the Jews for the war and all its problems.

3. She has been reading a great deal, particularly history; working out family trees of European royalty, learning French and English, collecting film stars pictures; studying mythology and arranging her stories; writing fairy tales and stories; learning the Bible; and she wants to write a book called The Secret Annexe.

4. The downstairs was broken into, and everyone was terribly afraid.

5. She got her first kiss.

6. She's talking about her and Peter finding each other and falling in love.

7. She believes politicians can do what they do only if ordinary people allow it to happen to them.

8. The letter she wrote to her father is what she considers the worst.

9. It is a gift because then a person has something to believe in.

10. Accept appropriate answers.

Option l: Unit Test (page 44)

Matching: 1. I 2. D 3. G 4. F 5. J 6. K 7. H 8. A 9. B 10. E 11. L 12. C

True or False: 1. False, 2. True, 3. True, 4. False, 5. True

Short Answer: 1. The Secret Annexe, 2. Mrs. Van Daan, 3. Amsterdam, 4. Mythology, film stars, writing, history, favors of European royalty, 5. disliked them intensely; did not understand how they could treat people the way they were treating the Jews

Essay: Accept all appropriate and well-supported responses.

©*1996 Teacher Created Materials, Inc.*